Five Things

poems by

Galen Steele

Finishing Line Press
Georgetown, Kentucky

Five Things

Copyright © 2025 by Galen Steele
ISBN 979-8-89990-293-2 First Edition
All rights reserved under International and Pan-American Copyright Conventions. No part of this book may be reproduced in any manner whatsoever without written permission from the publisher, except in the case of brief quotations embodied in critical articles and reviews.

ACKNOWLEDGMENTS

The book's title *Five Things* is drawn from Fr. Richard Rohr's "Five Essential Truths" in his book *Adam's Return*. The section titles are the five truths.

Grateful acknowledgment is made to the editor of *Fireflies' Light* for publishing "Combustion", "You saw Me Standing" in slightly altered form.

Thank you Shell for the inspiration to write.

Thank you Fort Worth Poetry Society for the discipline to play with words.

Thank you Suzanne for the courage to see it all through.

Publisher: Leah Huete de Maines
Editor: Christen Kincaid
Cover Art: Galen Steele
Author Photo: Jess Grady
Cover Design: Elizabeth Maines McCleavy

Order online: www.finishinglinepress.com
also available on amazon.com

Author inquiries and mail orders:
Finishing Line Press
PO Box 1626
Georgetown, Kentucky 40324
USA

Contents

I. Life Is Hard 1

The Way Back
Covering with Laughter
Regret in the Morning
Summer Tempest
My Algorithm: The Hailstone Sequence
Mother Like Son
Wounding Occurs Most Often
Golden Rule
Sanskrit for War
Finding What We Need
Envy
Places to Forget

II. You Are Not That Important 17

Recollections
Proudest Moment of the Fourth Grade
Wedding with Eyes on Me
Lessons in Obscurity
Small Heroes
Average
Creating Patterns
The Day After
Second Chances
The Future
Home Office

III. Your Life Is Not About You 31

Now That We Know Each Other
Devil's Hole
An Education
You Saw Me Standing
The Truth About Parenting
Word to the Wise
Bread of Life
Men
Making Plans with Mom
Missing
Communicative Intent

IV. You Are Not in Control 47

Arriving
The Greatest Sin
The Stars at Night
Some Kind of Reckoning
Trespassing
How Much More
Keeping Score
Cormorant Trees
Vanishing
Trying to Remember
Yesterday
Combustion

V. You Are Going to Die 63

The Process

Don't Look Back

Fine Print

Ornithology of Grief

An Abundance of Caution

With

Community

Insomnia

Imperative Moments Forgotten on Waking

Moths Are Nocturnal

The End

I. Life is Hard

Life is Hard

I could only afford the cheapest
items on the menu, but the short order cook
who on other days was also a plumber's apprentice
and a studio musician delighted in adding embellishments
to my burger so I dined like a king on kindness and grace.

Except for the night a process server
delivered a paternity suit filed by a woman
the cook met at a party in Memphis after recording.
"How will I explain this to my wife?" he asked
while handing me a dinner that tasted like tears.

The Way Back

Sorrow is the dirt where oil is spilt.
Lament is the digging until new life can grow.

Anger is a fire to burn your house down.
Lament is the spreading of ashes.

Fear is the winter frozen and cold.
Lament is the gathering of blankets.

Grief is the violent threshing in the field.
Lament is the winnowing of grain.

Loss is the distance from home.
Lament is the work of walking back.

Covering with Laughter

I keep pressing towards
something real,
but when I see it coming,
I jump out of the way.

"Tell the story again,"
she says, "but this time
tell it without laughing."

But it's funny, I insist

"Just try."

So I try—it's like
wearing paper clothes
in the rain.

Regret in the Morning

The pit of my stomach
has given way
to emptiness.
My body now ends
just above the waist.
My heart reclines
against my liver
and beats lazily,
smiling faintly at my
left lung grasping
at my ribs
just to stay in place.

"Where do you feel that
in your body?"
my therapist used to ask.
I didn't know then
what I know now.
Nor am I pleased
to have found
the answer.

Summer Tempest

The sky is not angry,
it is just out of breath
from traveling so far
to get here in time to blow
the hat off your head.

The sky is not unhappy,
it is just shaking itself dry
after plunging in exuberance
into the ocean
while on its way here.

The sky is not exasperated,
it is just singing the bass lines
in the celestial choir
making our chests rumble
like a boom car at the stoplight.

The sky is not threatening,
it is just lighting matches to find
the keys it lost in the dark
so it can go home to rest
for more adventure tomorrow.

My Algorithm: A Hailstone Sequence

> Once described as a soviet plot to distract serious mathematicians, the mystery is whether the hailstone sequence will end in the same loop for any starting value. The rules are this: if n is even, divide by 2. If n is odd multiply by three add one then divide by two. (A lotus has seven petals.)

The petals of Buddha's lotus flower
increased by the corners of the globe
again, less the fingers of your hand
a hat trick
    plus Goldilocks' bears,
        plus the Father, Son and Holy Ghost
diminished by unlucky Fridays
and a week later
less the Bill of Rights
then severed in two
include the deadly sins
    minus pride and lust,
        gluttony and sloth
spare my mom and dad, brother and sister
remove my dreams of glory, my visions of grandeur
and so only I remain
with you
I remain
with you
and I remain
with you…

Mother Like Son

I used to tease my mom
whose ample breasts gathered
crumbs from cookies,
splashes of broth from sampled soups,
or splotches of tomato sauce
flicked from the loose ends of noodles.

Now my belly plays the same role
acting as a scribe recording
all my daily indulgences
in Rorschach test patterns
on my last shirt
without a stain.

Wounding Occurs Most Often by Things that Never Happen

the friends that never call
the burdens never shared
the stories never told
the joys never expressed
the loneliness never quenched
the fights never voiced
the forgiveness never given
the love never spoken

Golden Rule

If there is another civil war
my neighbor will kill me.
I am the "them" to his "us,"
the Tutsi to his Hutu,
the Jew to his German.
I am the insidious cause
to his most grievous effect.

If there is an apocalypse
my other neighbor will kill me.
It will happen accidentally
once the marijuana is gone
but the munchies are not.
I will startle him when he
crawls through the window
his needing in search of my having.

If there is an ethnic cleansing
my neighbors and I will kill
the family across the street
because if there are only two sides
we prefer alive over dead.
It's not that we are monsters,
or racists–
It's just what neighbors do.

Sanskrit for War

Translates to English as
"to get more cows"

to gather more potatoes,
to accumulate more precious stones,
more status, more attention,
more sex, more quarters
for video games
and pizza
and beer,

to hoard more ribbon,
to gather more adornments,
more sugar, more spice,
more passion, more
whispered words for keeping warm
being cherished
feeling safe.

Which then is the cause of violence
is it "to get" or is it "more"?

Finding What We Need

My wife knows
where her organs are
and can find them
with her fingertips.

I am composed of skin
filled with guts
and the occasional rigid bone
none of which I can find
or even name.

My wife cannot find
the car in a parking lot,
and since the key battery died,
she has no way to call for help.

I know where my body is
in relation to the ordinal points
of the compass, in relation to the car,
to my way home, and even
the nearest body of water.

I don't care what happens
inside my flesh,
as long as I can find her body.

She doesn't care about
points on a map,
as long as she can hold me close.

Envy

I know a guy who lives a charmed life.
Reading a list of his achievements
is like reading a compilation
of all my broken dreams.

And while they say a rising tide lifts all boats,
it doesn't help if, like me, you are in a rowboat
on a dry lake bed in the perpetual desert.

And while they say it's no use making comparisons,
no one seems inclined to heed that advice around me,

so while he has not thought of me in years
I periodically spend a weekend hating his guts.

Places to Forget

I don't know the last time
I saw a deer around here,
but driving west towards Abilene
I saw six dead and bloated
by the side of the road
before reaching Weatherford.

I broke down once in Weatherford years ago
driving home from my honeymoon.
Our car coasted to a rest
right in front of a seedy hotel.
It wasn't clean or quiet,
and the TV only picked up CB chatter.

That was thirty years ago,
and I've never had a reason
to come back by until today,
and now I'm remembering exactly
why I stayed away
from this road where things die.

II. You Are Not That Important

You Are Not That Important

Having successfully defended my dissertation
and proudly taking the title *doctor*,
I walked past the library on the way to my car
and reflected on all the time I'd spent there
on the third floor, in the west wing,
down the 5th aisle hand resting on the center pillar,
scanning all the books I'd read on the second and third shelf.
All my accumulated knowledge, in a handful of tomes
barely enough to sustain a campfire
certainly not adequate
to burn the world down.

Recollections

I'm at the age now
when all stories I tell are long stories.
Lies are simple but the truth needs unpacking,
so I find myself referring farther and farther back
to discern points of demarcation
trying to recall the anti-meme version of how life is.

Knowledge is not a hermit.
It thrives in an abundance of friends,
and now, being so far removed,
memory operates like a book
read while daydreaming.
Fragments meld into parables
constructed in reverse.

Proudest Moment of the Fourth Grade

Mr. Siebum selected my poem to be read in a ceremony
at the only place that mattered. In rural Oregon,
nothing in our town was official until it happened at the mall.
To have my words read in those hallowed halls
was a gateway to immortality.

However, my elation was tempered by the keen awareness
that boys don't write poems, so I arranged for Sherri Duncan
to read my verse to the assembled throng on my behalf
while I, like an expectant father, stayed home.

She stood before the microphone on the stage
facing the Orange Julius where blenders growled
behind rows and rows of plastic fruit, and she
read my words to mothers who glanced longingly beyond
at the Dillard's window display.

She smiled as she read to fathers checking their watches
wondering if there might be time to swing through the tool aisle
at Sears before driving home.

She enunciated rhymes to boys who kept one eye
on the neon sign of the arcade and the other on the sweaty quarter
pinched between their thumb and forefinger.

She paused at the closing crescendo to maintain the spell over girls
who appeared to listen intently, their gaze transfixed
on the Buy-One-Get-One-Free poster at Claire's just visible over
Sherri's shoulder.

All the while I waited at home, my lips silently mouthing the words
as I recited them emphatically and passionately
from the shelter of my room, certain life was about to change.

Wedding with Eyes on Me

The tempura shrimp stared up out of the fried rice,
their black eyes vaguely pleading to me
over the shame of their predicament,

The pig seemed to snarl at the obligatory fruit
shoved between its teeth. Better he resent the apple
than me, as I tickled his ribs with a fork.

The platter of chicken was punctuated by bald heads
whose delicate beaks were poised to harshly judge
my selection with a rap to the back of my hand.

And if I thought the food gave me looks, I garnered
far more attention when I returned from the liquor store
to replenish the cognac which the groomsmen greedily consumed

well before the festivities began.

Lessons in Obscurity

In zombie movies, I am eaten in the opening scene
while trying to render aid before anyone realizes
what exactly is going on.

In high school sport movies,
I'm the blurry helmet at the back of the huddle,
or standing ready in the locker room just out of frame.

In the legal drama, I sit in the gallery
mesmerized, equally persuaded
by the lawyer's truths and lies.

I'm in the car under Godzilla's foot,
or stuck in the traffic jam caused
by the international spy's high-speed chase.

I live in a city vaporized by aliens,
on the planet victimized by the Death Star,
asleep on the beach when the tsunami comes,
just trying to make a living
when the sinkhole devours my office.

I'm the swipe left in the romcom,
missing the meet-cute
because of a painful urology appointment.

I'm not mentioned when the credits roll,
not invited to the premiere.

I wait until it's free on Hulu
to find myself in the crowd.

Small Heroes

Maybe victory is always
in the hands of hobbits.
It's the bespectacled goblins
who dream logistical solutions
who feed the starving
who load empty bowls
who manage the beasts
that trample violence.

Maybe peace is always
in the song of red cheeked gnomes.
It's the fingers of nimble dwarves
who reassemble broken dreams,
who tinker on the edges of grief,
who rekindle the joy of craftsmanship,
who establish the rhythms
that revive the mundane.

Average

As a child, I never once imagined
I might be ordinary.
I was maybe twenty-five before fully realizing
no one else was enamored with me.

I thought I'd excel at work, but now,
having been fired from one career,
and spending twenty years in another
falling just short of middle management,
I am resigned to my cubicle.

I figured I'd undertake great tasks,
but mostly I remodel old houses,
fix broken pool pumps, and endlessly
search through the garage for lost tools
to numb my mind from its aspiring.

I anticipated a life of greater certainty
only to discover two things for sure:
God is with me and God is with others
when I am with them,
and neither of these require more from me
than what I am.

Creating Patterns

In junior high
we took a field trip
to a commune, a tour which
I understand now
is a very Oregon
thing to do,

at the time,
living communally
in geodesic cabins
deep in the woods
with no sewer or electricity
seemed a perfectly normal
thing to do.

In support of our educational cause,
I was tasked with making vital
menu selections for our class lunch,
and thinking everyone would want
to try something exciting and new,
I chose the pumpkin soup
which in retrospect was not
the thing to do.

I endured the mockery.
I wore the scorn,
but now 37 years later
I select my annual pumpkin
to roast, spice, and puree
to make the perfect soup.
It's just a thing
I'm meant to do.

The Day After

There was blood here once.
Some sensitive neighbor
rinsed it away
with a garden hose,
with the same vigor I used
to scrub it off my knees.

Sticky maroon puddles,
clotting, coagulating in the heat.
I couldn't see the anguish
in his face, or the fear
in on-looking eyes.
I could only see
the persistent pulsing wound.

There is no rinsing
the fear from my mind,
no scrubbing away the anger
tight in my clenched teeth,
no restoring peace
to my now violent street.

The angst and prayer of strangers
who gathered near still lingers
in the fingertips of the trees,
The boy is still crumpled
where the bullet left him.
I still kneel vainly
trying to hold back
the blood.

Second Chances

I was 45 two years in a row
mostly because I lost count,
and no one else in my life
was paying any attention,

so when I took myself out to dinner
to celebrate turning 46,
I did the math and discovered
I had 12 months to go.

It is not often one is given
the opportunity to begin again,
but knowing my first pass was flawed
I eagerly grasped the second chance.

My dinner tasted better
seasoned with hindsight,
marking both my arrival,
and my fresh start.

The Future

I flip through blank pages of my journal
just checking to see if they hold any hints
about what will happen next.

It's the analog version of updating my feed.
The vague hope for a stray hit of dopamine,
and a particular hoping for secrets to be revealed.

I find a receipt tucked away between the pages,
but it's only for Dr. Pepper and Junior Mints
I bought and consumed weeks ago.

That's how the future is, I guess, littered with the detritus
of not so distant days where, sadly,
past performance is no guarantee of future returns.

Home Office

I tried to work,
but instead
I took a shower,
did laundry,
wrote a love note to my wife,
checked my email
played a game,
drank coffee,
took a walk,
sat on the toilet,
called my mom,
washed dishes,
checked the scores,
fed the dogs,
trimmed my beard,
packed a bag,
made lunch,
and wrote this poem.

If I work just as hard
this afternoon,
I may be able to catch a nap
before I call it a day.

# III. Your Life Is Not About You

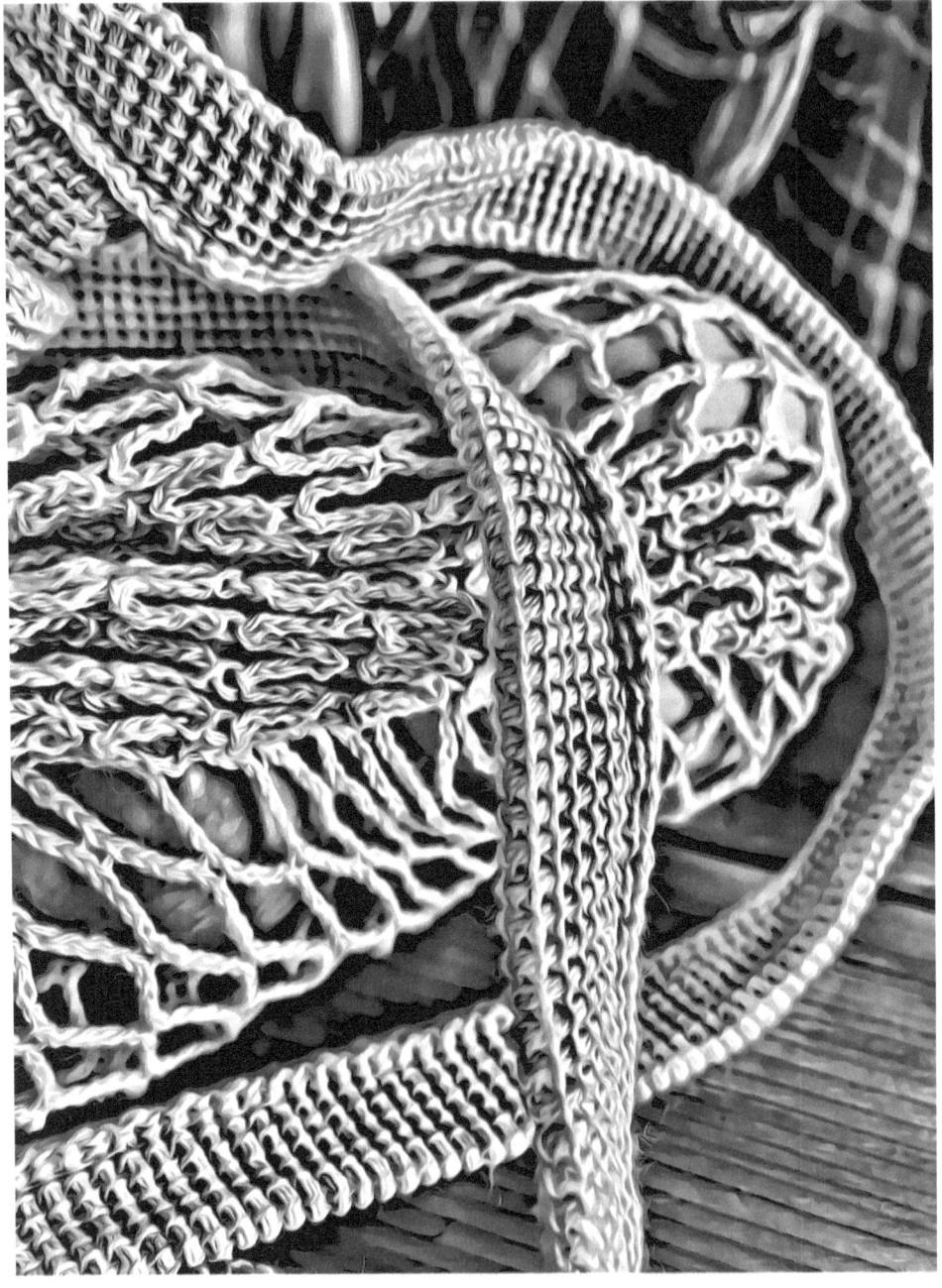

Your Life Is Not About You

"You can help by staying out of the way," my dad said.
I wandered outside so grandpa could watch his soaps,
and I played on the porch so grandma could cook.

In school I was picked last, so big kids could be sure to win.
My church served me platitudes because they had answers
they didn't want to share, or just because my intensity
made old ladies nervous.

I prayed to a God who only hoped I could sit still through the sermon,
and I was assured by the Bible that while some characters
are integral to the contours of history, I was not.

Now That We Know Each Other

"I think a little humility will go a long way
in solving your problem," you admonish,
and since you are never sarcastic,
I have no idea what you mean.
When I try to reply,
you have already moved on.

"I know you fancy yourself a Bono
but you are a David Byrne," you assert.
Your truth bombs are unsettling and alluring.
I don't think it is a dig,
and what if I am David Byrne?

Tonight, you adopted a new life motto
and I dropped everything to give you my full attention.
"Death comes for us all," you announced
followed by, "I'm going to brush my teeth."

In truth, I think you are not sure what's next
when your little gems find a soft target,
maybe you're just surprised I am listening.

Devil's Hole

In a neglected reservoir
in a corner of the world
God forgot to finish
where only dust
is more bountiful than sun
where wind mutters bitterly
for having to pass this way
where every living thing
is either scorched or chilled,
a furtive band of survivors lives.

In a fissure in a craggy rock,
in a valley named Death
lies a pond so small
one may leap across
where tiny blue fish
live and thrive
blissfully unaware
any universe exists
beyond their stone shelf
and the cold abyss below.

An Education

A Salvation Army General, an Indian Chief,
and a Water Sanitation Engineer walk into a classroom.
It might be the set up for a bad joke,
but they were my desk buddies
in a graduate class on public policy.

I lived with a heavily redacted Bible in my head
that only included verses about sin and judgment.
So I greeted each of them with suspicion, and they,
with their own edited texts, returned the skepticism.

From her holy perch in the office of the homeless shelter,
the General struggled to balance her limitless compassion
for the downtrodden with her cynical disdain
for their choices. She reminded us continually,
Jesus loved the poor and forgotten
although she rarely remembered why.

The Chief carried generations of his people's pain
bound in the tight knots of his braid.
He knew words were only cheap tricks.
That treaties give and courts take away.
In a room inclined to champion his cause,
he returned every kind word
with the clenched fists of oppression.

With the security of position and a pension
the Engineer earnestly implored for adherence
to the process, "for the greatest good."
Blissfully unaware processes might be broken,
oblivious that procedure can kill.
Forgetting slavery, internment camps,
and the Trail of Tears were all led by
good Americans following the rules.

And I, hearing their hearts, surrendered my judgment.
Accepting their anguish, put away my eye for sin.
Realizing if there was a joke, it was on me,
so walking home I tossed aside
my well-worn scriptures
to try again.

You Saw Me Standing

in a place I already was.
You heard me singing
a song you already knew.
You just arrived where
I've been waiting all my life.
I only now discovered wisdom
you have written on your wall.
Did we discover this love,
or have we invented something new?

The Truth About Parenting

The lies I told
were for your benefit.
Hard bits of sageness
to keep stuck in your skin
like goat head burrs.

These lies I repeated
never knowing truth
beyond their sting.
These bits of wisdom
easier to live than believe.

Forgive me for
the lies that bind us
through accidents of birth.
Remove this spike from my flesh.
I'll remove the thorn from yours.

Word to the Wise

"Smoke follows beauty,"
aunt Jean often said from her perch
near the campfire and believing her to be wise
I pondered this power of beauty.

When the wind shifted, stinging my eyes with smoke,
I was confused. Did it know something of me
that I didn't know of myself?

"Age before beauty," aunt Jean always said
when passing with someone through a doorway,
although age seemed a less vital consideration.

When my time came to hold open the door
I was never quite clear if everyone knew their ranking,
or if it was mine to determine.

Bread of Life

An unhoused man I know
likes to collect day-old bread
from local bakeries to distribute
to those in need.

He slips into the quad of the local seminary
while behind closed doors
sermons are preached, Bibles exegeted,
and students theorize about
how to love their neighbors,
and cherish those near the heart of God.

Silently he goes about his work
filling the table then turning with a jerk,
and writing on a small card "Free."
His eyes twinkle with mischief,
cheeks redden with joy,
and in a flash, he disappears down the alley,

never staying to see the young scholars
flood the courtyard and greedily snatch up
loaves of bread, boxes of donuts, bags of bagels,
buns and biscuits all carefully provided
by the least of these.

Men

I watched a scary movie
which I almost never do.

The shape-shifting villain
was a metaphor for patriarchy,

and it harried a young woman
in search of herself.

I mean the adversary was literally
a metaphor so you can imagine

just how unstoppable it was.
Although we don't see

how the protagonist
finally defeats it,

either she kills it with an ax
or points out its logical fallacies.

No matter how it happened
I locked all the doors,

and was much more careful
about the things I said to whom.

Making Plans with Mom

"Well, I really wanted to attend my 60th high school reunion, but no one thinks I should drive that far."

I'll drive you, mom.

"Well, I really wanted to go to Oregon to visit my old friends, but there isn't enough time."

I'll arrange a week in Oregon, mom.

"Well, I've lost interest in traveling, what I really want is someone to help me in the garden."

Have you called my brother?

Missing

I'm missing a button today
which I would have noticed earlier
if I had finished dressing at home
and not in the parking lot at work.

It's my belly button,
not my umbilical receptor
but the button marking
the outer limit of my girth.

Maybe I'll imitate Napoleon
tucking my hand into my shirt
where the button ought to be.

Or I can dress down, going fully
unbuttoned and untucked.

Or more likely, I will just cease to notice
and I will blend into the bland walls
where I am generally overlooked
despite my public blemishes.

Communicative Intent

This cantankerous old crow
keeps announcing his presence
with clicks and caws and cackles.

I stare trying to read his lips
certain there is communicative intent,
but for whom and to what end?

It is not unlike this ink
scrawled across the paper
never to be seen.

What is the intent
of words never spoken
like the sound of a crow
in the wind?

IV. You Are Not in Control

You Are Not in Control

Somewhere in the vast shantytown
of tin-roofed shacks and hovels,
I dug a latrine into the earth.
The sides crumbled dry
like bright orange embers.
I relished the cool of my hole,
and the quiet search for answers.
My pick and shovel the limit of my control
until even the handles broke
leaving only me and dirt.

Arriving

The silver image glimmers
on the bright horizon.
The first ripple of the sea
or last bending of the sky.

A thousand questions fall silent
onto the floor boards
slowly stirred by
the vibrating gear stick.

Our blue Dodge pickup
unrolls the ribbon of road,
chasing the mirage oasis
another hundred miles.

The windows, wide open.
The curve of my hand
riding the currents
of warm pulsing wind.

"It's not far now," my dad said,
speaking for the first time in hours.
We spent our days driving,
but arriving, we never did.

The Greatest Sin

is to ask a pious person
for an apology.

There are six things
the self-righteous despise;
seven they find detestable:
the sin of strangers,
transparency,
an inquisitive spirit,
the chaos of relationship,
mystery, feet that dance,
and the audacity of love.

The Stars at Night

I can see the Milky Way from here
or as my friend likes to point out,
I can see the Milky Way as it was
a gazillion years ago.
I don't know if that makes it
more or less special.

It is the same friend who tells me
the cells that became me originated
in the body of my grandmother
because my mother's eggs were already
assembled before she was born.
I find this fascinating and mortifying
considering I was nearly fifty before
becoming aware of my body at all,
and I'm not ready to know
where my cells have been without me.

I believe a modicum of ignorance
is essential to maintain a normal life.
I don't need to know there are bugs in my food,
or that I'm drinking the same water as Napoleon.
I just want to look in the sky,
and say, "Wow, the Milky Way."

Some Kind of Reckoning

I fell asleep as the wind pixelated the windows with rain
zeros and ones at first static then running together down the glass
as the sky's ragged breath howled through gaps in the door
as timpani drums beat asynchronously to illuminating pulses of light.

Silence woke me later. The sound of water seeping into stone,
of cacti swelling, of crickets shaking themselves dry,
of cicadas counting beats quietly until sunrise,
of night creatures curling a little tighter in nooks and burrows
now over damp on the edges.

And there is no path forward, as even time pauses to gather its breath
preen its feathers, and imagine what might grow beyond this cool reprieve,
beyond the golden shadow of trees now littering the lawn,
beyond the inhaled breath of this stormy night.

Trespassing

"These were planted
by Johnny Appleseed,"
I whispered reverently.

In the woods, this hidden sanctum
near my childhood home,
tucked between the oaks and firs,

a dozen apple trees grew
standing apart, a humble huddle,
a feral, knobby orchard.

The fruit was small, green,
fiercely tart, and densely packed
on drooping branches.

Apples in the woods
are an invitation
not unlike cottages made of candy,

but the unpruned limbs
bristle with warning
this blessing is not meant for you.

How Much More

I slept just enough to be awake now
but not enough to make it through the day.

I've earned just enough to have my daily bread,
but not enough to feed my dreams of rest.

I've learned just enough to stay out of trouble,
but not enough to disrupt patterns that devour.

I've loved just enough to know what is possible,
but not enough to pass it on to my neighbor.

Just enough
is not enough,
on every score
I'm needing something more.

Keeping Score

Bad things happen in threes,
but sometimes I invent the third thing,
just to make it stop.

Great things may happen in threes too,
but I'm less stingy about those,
often losing count.

There is no limit to mundane moments.
I tried to count them once, but they are points on a line,
countless tiny infinities.

Cormorant Trees

At dusk, the barren trees
fill with plump, feathered fruit
like persimmons clinging to the boughs
long after the leaves have gone.

Their conversations are muted
by the river rumbling through the rocks.
In the long shadows the sunfish
and catfish and bass finally breathe easy
now hidden from the eyes above.
Only the otter casts them a wary glance
from the tall grasses on the shallow shoreline.

The plump morsels periodically fall, reconsider,
and return, waiting to be plucked up
by dreams riding on the evening breeze.

Vanishing

Sometimes I stop reading,
but my eyes continue to clamor
across the bumps and ridges,
and leap over gaps and indents,
finishing off paragraphs and pages
while I…I have no idea where I go.
Perhaps there's some happy place in my mind
where I am heroic, or where life is predictable,
or truth is simple and lies are plain.

Sometimes I arrive home from work
having no idea how I got there.
I drove, obviously, but I have no recall
of traffic, no memory of songs or radio news.

Sometimes I leave the conversation
while bobbing my head,
still muttering "oh" and "yeah"
but I'm not listening, not preparing a response.
It's like I have fallen between the parentheses
and can't get up.

I vanish into the stream of consciousness
of the ever-expanding universe
until forced back to the place I left
slightly tired and confused
trying to recall where all this was heading
when I left sometime last week.

Trying to Remember

I just heard a poem
and I'm trying to write it down
verbatim from memory.

So far I only remember
three words:
body, pencil, and Jesus.

Maybe not in that particular order.

I assume Jesus could write with a pencil
if they had yellow number twos
with pink erasers back then.

Certainly Jesus had a body,
and if I was nearby
I'd probably poke him constantly

just like I poke my wife
at night to make sure
she is still there.

Yesterday

There is a fly in my room.
I can't tell if he is slow
or just lazy.

I brush him to the side
so I can set down my cup,
and he tumbles off the nightstand
only taking flight after bouncing
off a book on the floor.

The book is Just Kids
by Patti Smith.
Maybe he only wanted
a closer look.
Maybe he is a fan.

Laboriously he rises
bumping at intervals against the wall
until he reaches the molding above the closet
where he sits.

I swear I hear him panting
or maybe, like my dogs,
he has fallen asleep
and is actively dreaming
of a day like yesterday
when he was a kid.

Combustion

Lightning bugs in the willow branches
set trees on fire at dusk.

Where the milkweed is trampled near the trail,
monarchs melt the ground,
a roiling cauldron of orange and black.

Ladybugs light flares on the stems of wild dill.

While cicadas and crickets conspire
rubbing ribs and legs to kindle a flame
to burn up the night.

V. You Are Going to Die

You Are Going to Die

The afternoon before my wedding
the groomsmen went to the river to swim
and dared me to jump from a high rock
into the raging water below,
and for the first time I can recall,
I consciously changed my behavior
to avoid death.

The Process

First something happens.
It is either good or bad.
We conspire
to make it happen again
or make it stop.

Next, something else happens,
and it is either better or worse
than before
which is an introduction
to either pride or regret.

Finally, the last thing happens,
and we run back
to the end of the line
hoping we have enough tickets
to do it all again.

Don't Look Back

Orpheus looked back.
Was it joy or doubt?
Either way,
it was only fleeting
compared to the painful shout.

Lot's wife looked back.
Was it regret or fear?
Either way,
it was an instant
marked in salt right here.

I looked back.
Was it dismay or wonder?
Either way,
it was the moment
I finally slipped under.

Fine Print

According to the apostle Paul,
there is no sex in heaven.
It is in the Bible,
but seldom mentioned
in Sunday sermons
because one might be inclined
to question the value of self-control
if the only reward is
a much longer abstinence.

According to Muslim scholars
the whole 72 virgins as a reward
for faithful martyrs
may be a mistranslation.
The promise is likely
just bunches of white grapes.
This could prove disappointing
but less frustrating
if, in fact, there is no sex
in paradise.

Ornithology of Grief

In the weeks after my father-in-law died,
a cardinal began rapping at his wife's window.

"I think that's Bob coming back to visit me,"
she said. "He comes every morning just to say hello."

So a year later when we're all gathered for Christmas,
I wasn't surprised to hear the rat-a-tat-tat
of a cardinal at the window.

"Bob is here," I said.
"Oh, that's not Bob," she scolds, "that's my brother."

An Abundance of Caution

Russian troops in Afghanistan
had access to local markets
but very little money.

What they did have were bullets
which local vendors accepted
as readily as cash.

Wanting to trade,
but not wanting to be killed
by their own black-market ammo,

soldiers boiled their bullets
hoping to make them inert
before trading.

I do the same thing
before angry rants.
Boiling away the venom

before I speak
so my words don't come back
to kill me.

With

Maybe I'm the prodigal son
you never had.

Maybe I've come from the gutter
where only pigs feed.

Maybe I'm returning to grace
offered but not received.

Maybe I've come to tell you
I heard you even then.

Maybe I'm just grateful
to be home.

Community

I tended to a neighbor boy
shot in the leg during a fight.
Nearby, dressed in the prim
uniform of a grandma,
Mrs. Monroe surveyed the scene
then disappeared into her house,
and returned with a long Harry Potter scarf
of crimson and gold.
She wrapped it around his leg,
twisted it as tight as elderly hands would allow.

I couldn't tell her
the bullet hole
was in the other leg.

Insomnia

It's three hours until dawn
and this wakeful twilight has stretched on
longer than the forty winks cut short by a slamming door.

Rest has scrubbed my mind clean
while fatigue keeps the lists of morning at bay,
a limbo holding me in a trance.

It is the gap between dry and sober,
exhaustion and collapse,
achievement and resignation,

These liminal moments nip at my resolve
like an angry goose, like a dog unchained,
like a chatty drunk.

And I lie here vacillating between what I hope for
and what I can get. Gray is the predecessor of the rainbow,
the harbinger of kindness or the first strokes of oblivion,

and I won't know for sure until my alarm arouses me
from wakefulness to bury my thoughts
with repetitive rhythms of doing and dying.

Imperative Moments Forgotten on Waking

I put a metaphor in my pocket,
but it melted on the way home
seeping through my pants
declaring an accident, when really
only exuberance and inattention collided.

Similes are stones I roll
between my fingers and thumb
before I throw them into conversation
just to see how you will react.
Your expression is the photo in my mind.

The balm of allegory relieves wounds
I've carried but forgotten.
Its touch is electric, incomprehensible,
but I rest in the knowledge
healing is contagious.

Moths Are Nocturnal

They are to butterflies
what bats are to birds.
They are what rats are to squirrels,
what crickets are to grasshoppers,
what nightmares are to daydreams,
what waiting is to doing,
what stars are to the sun,
what black is to blue,
what snores are to songs,
and they perish
mistaking the moon
and the flame.

The End

I received a notice in the mail,
the world is ending Thursday night.
Sadly I just opened the letter,
and it's already Tuesday morning.

I'll definitely call in sick tomorrow,
and probably Thursday too.
I'd run out and do something special,
but I don't get paid till Friday next.

I'd like to go a little wild,
or stay at home and have more sex,
but our walls are paper thin,
and the kids are out of school.

I have books I'd like to finish,
but I guess there is no point in that.
There are poems I'd like to write
but I guess I'm just a fool.

Maybe I'll walk with Michelle
counting feral cats.
We can eat leftovers from the fridge,
and Thursday night we can say,

we made it to the end.

Galen Steele has lived many lives including stays in Oregon, Washington, California and Texas with careers in financial services and teaching (high school math and college political science). He enjoys being a proud father, a squirrelly son, a weird uncle, a rambunctious friend, and a grateful husband.

He amuses himself by scribbling poems into the margins of contracts, reports, and church bulletins. He writes poetry, memoir, and the occasional play. His prior work has been published in *Fireflies' Light* and *A Book of the Year* for the Poetry Society of Texas. He makes his own paper and binds his own books but doesn't have many shelves left to fill.

www.ingramcontent.com/pod-product-compliance
Lightning Source LLC
Chambersburg PA
CBHW020831190426
43197CB00037B/1542